THE PIED PIPER of HAMELIN

ORCHARD BOOKS
96 Leonard Street, London EC2A 4RH
Orchard Books Australia
14 Mars Road, Lane Cove, NSW 2066
ISBN 1 85213 651 0 (paperback)
ISBN 1 85213 414 3 (hardback)
First published in Great Britain 1993
First paperback publication 1994
Illustrations © André Amstutz 1993 ·
The right of André Amstutz to be indentified as the illustrator of this work has
been asserted by him in accordance with the Copyright, Designs and Patents Act, 1988.
A CIP catalogue record for this book is available from the British Library.
Printed in Belgium
9 10 8

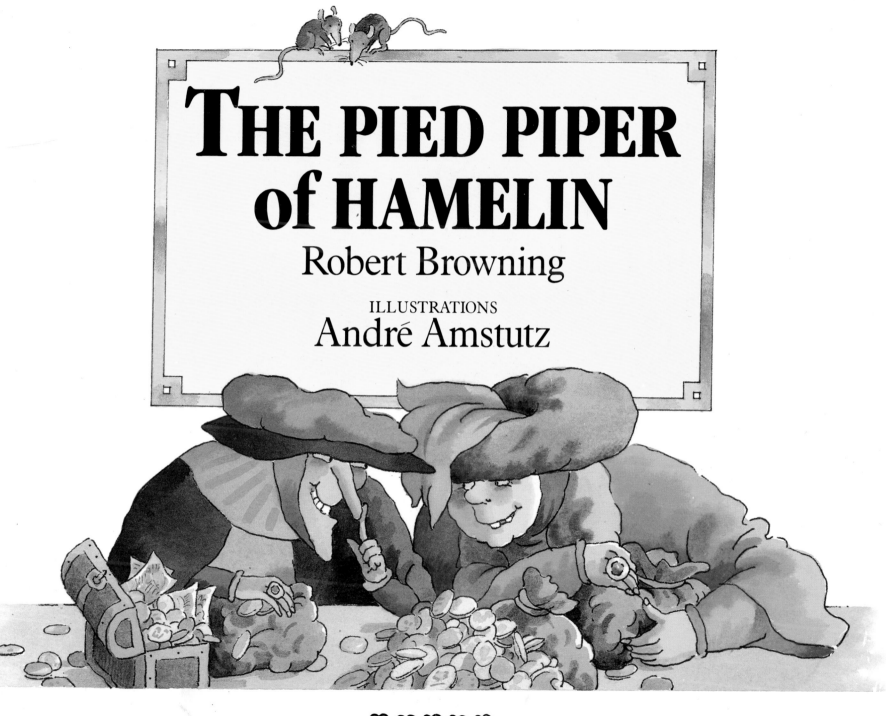

THE PIED PIPER
of HAMELIN

Robert Browning

ILLUSTRATIONS
André Amstutz

ORCHARD BOOKS

Hamelin Town's in Brunswick,
By famous Hanover city;
The River Weser, deep and wide,
Washes its wall on the southern side;
A pleasanter spot you never spied;
But when begins my ditty,
Almost five hundred years ago
To see townsfolk suffer so
From vermin, was a pity.

Rats!
They fought the dogs,
And killed the cats,
And bit the babies
In the cradles,
And ate the cheeses
Out of the vats,
And licked the soup
From the cooks' own ladles,
Split open the kegs
Of salted sprats,
Made nests inside
Men's Sunday hats,
And even spoiled
The women's chats,
By drowning their speaking
With shrieking
And squeaking
In fifty different
Sharps and flats.

At last the people in a body
To the Town Hall came flocking:
"Rouse up, Sirs!
Give your brains a racking
To find the remedy we're lacking,
Or, sure as fate,
We'll send you packing!"
At this the Mayor and Corporation
Quaked with a mighty consternation.

An hour they sat in council,
At length the Mayor broke silence:
"It's easy to bid one rack one's brain –
I'm sure my poor head aches again
I've scratched it so, and all in vain.
Oh for a trap, a trap, a trap!"
Just as he said this, what should hap
At the chamber door but a gentle tap?
"Come in!" the Mayor cried,
Looking bigger.
And in did come the strangest figure!

His queer long coat from heel to head
Was half of yellow and half of red;
And he himself was tall and thin,
With sharp blue eyes, each like a pin,
And light loose hair, yet swarthy skin,
No tuft on cheek nor beard on chin,
And nobody could enough admire
The tall man and his quaint attire.
He advanced to the council-table.
And, "Please your honours,"
Said he, "I'm able,
By means of a secret charm, to draw
All creatures living beneath the sun,
After me so as you never saw!

And I chiefly use my charm
On creatures that do people harm,
The mole, the toad, and newt, and viper;
And people call me the Pied Piper.
If I can rid your town of rats
Will you give me one thousand guilders?"
"One? fifty thousand!"
Was the exclamation
Of the astonished Mayor
And Corporation.

Into the street the Piper stepped,
Smiling first a little smile,
As if he knew what magic slept
In his quiet pipe the while;
Then, like a musical adept,
To blow the pipe his lips he wrinkled,
And green and blue his sharp eyes twinkled
Like a candle flame where salt is sprinkled;
And ere three shrill notes the pipe uttered,
You heard as if an army muttered;
And the muttering grew to a grumbling;
And the grumbling grew to a mighty rumbling;
And out of the houses the rats came tumbling:

Great rats, small rats, lean rats, brawny rats,
Brown rats, black rats, grey rats, tawny rats,
Grave old plodders, gay young friskers,
Fathers, mothers, uncles, cousins,
Cocking tails and pricking whiskers,
Families by tens and dozens,
Brothers, sisters, husbands, wives,
Followed the Piper for their lives.

From street to street he piped advancing,
And step for step they followed dancing,
Until they came to the river Weser,
Wherein all plunged and perished –
Save one who lived to carry
To Rat-land home his commentary.

You should have heard the Hamelin people
Ringing the bells till they rocked the steeple;
"Go," cried the Mayor, "and get long poles!
Poke out the nests and block up the holes!
Consult with carpenters and builders,
And leave in our town not even a trace
Of the rats!" when suddenly up the face
Of the Piper perked in the market-place,
   With a
   "First,
   If you please,
   My thousand guilders!"

A thousand guilders! The Mayor looked blue;
So did the Corporation too.
To pay this sum to a wandering fellow
With a gipsy coat of red and yellow!
"Beside," quoth the Mayor with a knowing wink,
"Our business was done at the river's brink;
We saw with our eyes the vermin sink,
And what's dead can't come to life, I think.
But, as for guilders, what we spoke
Of them, as you well know, was in joke.
Beside, our losses have made us thrifty;
A thousand guilders! Come, take fifty!"

The Piper's face fell, and he cried,
"No trifling! I can't wait, beside!
And folks who put me in a passion
May find me pipe to another fashion."
"How?" cried The Mayor,
"D'ye think I'll brook
Being worse treated than a cook?
You threaten us, fellow? Do your worst,
Blow your pipe there till you burst!"

Once more he stepped into the street;
And to his lips again
Laid his long pipe of smooth straight cane;
And ere he blew three notes (such sweet
Soft notes as yet musician's cunning
Never gave the enraptured air)
There was a rustling,
That seemed like a bustling,
Of merry crowds justling
At pitching and hustling,
Small feet were pattering,
Wooden shoes clattering.
Little hands clapping,
And little tongues chattering.
And, like fowls in a farmyard
When barley is scattering,
Out came the children running.

All the little boys and girls,
With rosy cheeks and flaxen curls,
And sparkling eyes and teeth like pearls,
Tripping and skipping,
Ran merrily after
The wonderful music
With shouting and laughter.

The Mayor was dumb,
And the Council stood
As if they were changed
Into blocks of wood,
Unable to move a step, or cry
To the children merrily skipping by –
And could only follow with the eye
That joyous crowd at the Piper's back.

But how the Mayor was on the rack,
And the wretched Council's bosoms beat,
As the Piper turned from the High Street
To where the Weser rolled its waters
Right in the way of their sons and daughters!
However he turned from South to West,
And to Koppelberg Hill his steps addressed,

And after him the children pressed;
Great was the joy in every breast.
"He never can cross that mighty top!
He's forced to let the piping drop,
And we shall see our children stop!"
When, lo, as they reached the mountain's side,
A wondrous portal opened wide,
As if a cavern was suddenly hollowed;
And the Piper advanced and the children followed,
And when all were in to the very last,
The door in the mountain side shut fast.

Did I say, all? No! One was lame,
And could not dance the whole of the way.

And in after years, if you would blame
His sadness, he was used to say,
"It's dull in our town since my playmates left!
I can't forget that I'm bereft
Of all the pleasant sights they see,
Which the Piper also promised me;
For he led us, he said, to a joyous land
Joining the town and just at hand,
Where waters gushed and fruit trees grew,
And everything was strange and new;
The sparrows were brighter than peacocks here,
And their dogs outran our fallow deer
And honey bees had lost their stings,
And horses were born with eagles' wings;
And just as I became assured
My lame foot would be speedily cured
The music stopped and I stood still
And found myself outside the hill
Left alone against my will,
To go limping as before,
And never hear of that country more!"

Alas, alas for Hamelin!
The Mayor sent East, West, North, and South
To offer the Piper by word of mouth,
Wherever it was men's lot to find him,
Silver and gold to his heart's content,
If he'd only return the way he went,
And bring the children behind him.

But when they saw 'twas a lost endeavour,
And Piper and dancers were gone for ever
The place of the children's last retreat,
They called it, the Pied Piper's Street –
Where anyone playing on pipe or tabor
Was sure for the future to lose his labour.
Nor suffered they hostelry or tavern

To shock with mirth a street so solemn;
But opposite the place of the cavern
They wrote the story on a column,
And on the great church window painted
The same, to make the world acquainted
How their children were stolen away.
And there it stands to this very day.

This book belongs to:

We hope you enjoy this book.
Please return or renew it by the due date.
You can renew it at **www.norfolk.gov.uk/libraries**
or by using our free library app. Otherwise you can
phone **0344 800 8020** - please have your library
card and pin ready.
You can sign up for email reminders too.

NORFOLK COUNTY COUNCIL
LIBRARY AND INFORMATION SERVICE

NORFOLK ITEM

3 0129 08838 8567

Based on the episode "Paddington and the Pet Show" by James Lamont and Jon Foster

Adapted by Lauren Holowaty

First published in the United Kingdom by HarperCollins *Children's Books* in 2023
HarperCollins *Children's Books* is a division of HarperCollins*Publishers* Ltd
1 London Bridge Street
London SE1 9GF

www.harpercollins.co.uk

HarperCollins*Publishers*
Macken House, 39/40 Mayor Street Upper
Dublin 1, D01 C9W8, Ireland

1 3 5 7 9 10 8 6 4 2

ISBN: 978-0-00-856808-5

Printed in Great Britain by Bell and Bain Ltd, Glasgow

Based on the Paddington novels written and created by Michael Bond

PADDINGTON™ and PADDINGTON BEAR™ © Paddington and Company/STUDIOCANAL S.A.S. 2023
Paddington Bear™ and Paddington™ and PB™ are trademarks of Paddington and Company Limited
Licensed on behalf of STUDIOCANAL S.A.S. by Copyrights Group

This book is produced from independently certified FSC™ paper
to ensure responsible forest management.

For more information visit: www.harpercollins.co.uk/green